Can I Kick It?

Teaching Tips

Red Level 2

This book focuses on the phonemes /c/k/.

Before Reading

- Discuss the title. Ask readers what they think the book will be about.
- Sound out the words on page 3 together.

Read the Book

- Ask readers to use a finger to follow along with each word as it is read.
- Encourage readers to break down unfamiliar words into units of sound. Then, ask them to string the sounds together to create the words.
- Urge readers to point out when the focused phonics phonemes appear in the text.

After Reading

- Encourage children to reread the book independently or with a friend.
- Ask simple questions about the text to check for understanding. Have them find the pages that have the answers to your questions.

© 2024 Booklife Publishing
This edition is published by arrangement with Booklife Publishing.

North American adaptations © 2024 Jump!
5357 Penn Avenue South
Minneapolis, MN 55419
www.jumplibrary.com

Decodables by Jump! are published by Jump! Library.
All rights reserved. No part of this book may be reproduced in any form without written permission from the publisher.

Library of Congress Cataloging-in-Publication Data is available at www.loc.gov or upon request from the publisher.

ISBN: 979-8-88996-786-6 (hardcover)
ISBN: 979-8-88996-787-3 (paperback)
ISBN: 979-8-88996-788-0 (ebook)

Photo Credits

Images are courtesy of Shutterstock.com. With thanks to Getty Images, Thinkstock Photo and iStockphoto. Cover – JR-50. 4–5 – Slatan, Mega Pixel. 6–7 – Johannes Kornelius, Gelpi. 8–9 – Designs Stock, Microgen. 10–11 – Melle V, Juver. 15 – Shutterstock.

Can you find these words in the book?

can

kick

rock

Can I kick the can?

Can

I can kick the can.

Can I kick a rock?

Rock

No, I cannot kick a rock.

Can I kick the big bag?

I can kick the big bag.

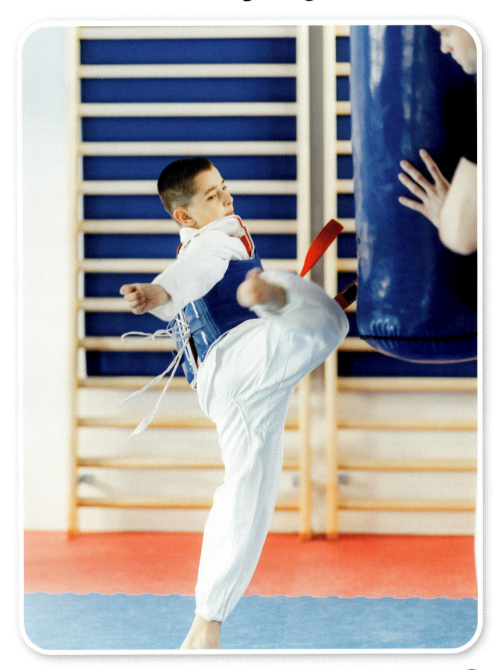

Can I kick the mud?

I did kick the mud.

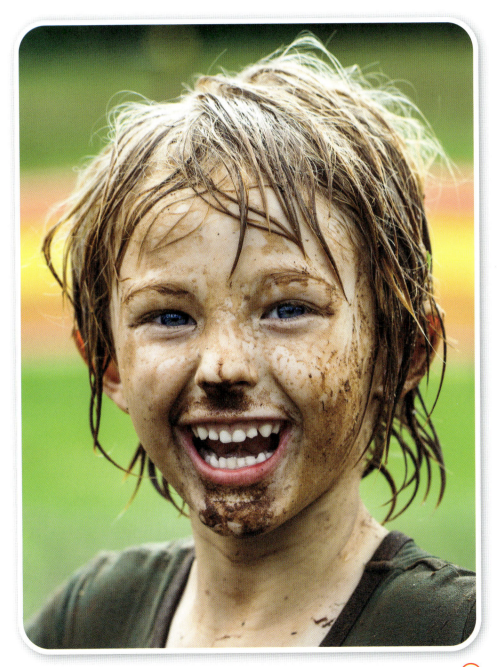

Can you say these sounds and draw them with your finger?

Using the Letter Bank, trace the missing letter into each word.

__ick

r__ck

__an

mu__

Letter Bank

c k o d

What other words do you know with the letters /c/ or /k/?

bucket

key

pack

Practice reading the book again:

Can I kick the can?
I can kick the can.
Can I kick a rock?
No, I cannot kick a rock.
Can I kick the big bag?
I can kick the big bag.
Can I kick the mud?
I did kick the mud.